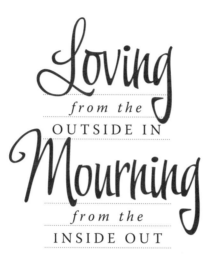

Loving
from the
OUTSIDE IN
Mourning
from the
INSIDE OUT

Companion Press is dedicated to the education and support
of both the bereaved and bereavement caregivers. We believe that
those who companion the bereaved by walking with them as they
journey in grief have a wondrous opportunity: to help others
embrace and grow through grief—and to lead fuller, more
deeply-lived lives themselves because of this important ministry.

For a complete catalog and ordering information, write, call, or visit:

Companion Press
The Center for Loss and Life Transition
3735 Broken Bow Road
Fort Collins, CO 80526
(970) 226-6050
www.centerforloss.com

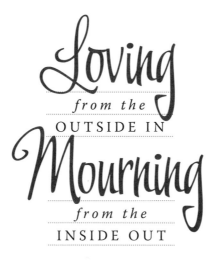

Loving
from the
OUTSIDE IN
Mourning
from the
INSIDE OUT

ALAN D. WOLFELT, PH.D.

Companion
P R E S S

An imprint of the Center for Loss and Life Transition
Fort Collins, Colorado

Companion Press is an imprint of the Center for Loss and Life Transition, 3735 Broken Bow Road, Fort Collins, Colorado 80526.

Printed in Canada

21 20 19 18 17 16 15 14 13   6 5 4 3 2

ISBN: 978-1-617221-47-7

IN
Gratitude

I hope this little book on love and grief is as useful
to you as writing it has been to me. I am grateful to
all of the people in my life who have taught me that
love and grief are birthrights of life and two sides of
the same coin. In particular, I am most grateful for
the love I share with my lovely wife, Susan, and my
three precious children, Megan, Chris, and Jaimie.
These four people give me so much to live for each
and every day I am on this earth.

Contents

Introduction

THE CAPACITY TO LOVE REQUIRES THE NECESSITY TO MOURN

"*Every time we make the decision to love someone, we open ourselves to great suffering, because those we most love cause us not only great joy but also great pain. The greatest pain comes from leaving...the pain of the leaving can tear us apart.*

"*Still, if we want to avoid the suffering of leaving, we will never experience the joy of loving. And love is stronger than fear, life stronger than death, hope stronger than despair. We have to trust that the risk of loving is always worth taking.*"

—Henri J.M. Nouwen

A very wise person once observed, "Love is not an option but a necessity." I couldn't agree more. We come into the world yearning to give and receive love. Authentic love is God's greatest gift to us as human beings. Love is the one human experience that invites us to feel beautifully connected and forces us to acknowledge that meaning and purpose are anchored not in isolation and aloneness, but in union and togetherness.

What higher purpose is there in life but to give and receive love? Love is the essence of a life of abundance and joy. No matter what life brings our way, love is our highest goal, our most passionate quest. Yes, we have a tremendous need for love—love that captures our hearts and nourishes our spirits.

In fact, our capacity to give and receive love is what ultimately defines us. Nothing we have "accomplished" in our lifetimes matters as much as the way we have loved one another. Love is a magical energy that is the very anchor, substance, and essence of life.

This naturally leads me to the theme of this book: *the capacity to love requires the necessity to mourn*. I write this resource from my unique perspective as a grief counselor and educator. It is an invitation to help you honor both your love and your need to mourn when someone you love dies. No matter the type of relationship—whether the person who died was your parent, lover, spouse, child, or friend—my hope is that this book speaks to your heart and soul. You may also find this book helpful where someone has left your life through divorce or some other form of transition. To honor means to "recognize the value of and respect," and both your continued love and your grief need this recognition and attention from you right now.

You see, love and grief are two sides of the same precious coin. One does not—and cannot—exist without the other. They are the yin and yang of our lives. People sometimes say that grief is the price we pay for the joy of having loved. This also means, of course, that grief is not a universal experience. While I wish it were, sadly it is not. Grief is predicated on our capacity to give and receive love. Some people choose not to love and so never grieve. If we allow ourselves the grace that comes with love, however, we must allow ourselves the grace that is required to mourn.

The experience of grief is only felt when someone of great value, purpose, and meaning has been a part of your life. To mourn your loss is required if you are to befriend the love you have been granted. To honor your grief is not self-destructive or harmful, it is life-sustaining and life-giving, and it ultimately leads you back to love again. In this way, love is both the cause and the antidote.

Yes, it is a given that there is no love without loss. Likewise, there is no integration of loss without the experience of mourning. To deny the significance of mourning would be to believe that there is something wrong about loving. Just as our greatest gift from God is our capacity to give and receive love, it is a great gift that we can openly mourn our life losses.

It is important that you understand that grief and mourning are not the same thing, however. *Grief* is the constellation of thoughts and feelings we have when someone we love dies. We can think of it as the container. It holds our thoughts, feelings, and images of our experience when someone we love dies. In other words, grief is the internal meaning given to the experience of loss. *Mourning* is when we take the grief we have on the inside and express it outside of ourselves. Another way of defining mourning is "grief gone public" or "the outward expression of grief."

Making the choice to not just grieve but authentically mourn provides us the courage to live through the pain of loss and be transformed by it. How ironic that to ultimately go on to live well and love well we must allow ourselves to mourn well. Somewhere in the collision between the heart, which searches for permanency and connection, and the brain, which acknowledges separation and loss, there is a need for all of us to authentically mourn.

Just as you are well-served to honor love when you discover it, you are also well-served to honor your need to mourn in the face of loss. The thoughts on love and loss contained in this book are intended to help you do just that. They are designed to help you give honor in ways that allow you to openly and honestly mourn, even as your love never dies.

Yes, when you experience lost love, you are confronted with the need to mourn the loss, while consciously valuing what you have taken in, or internalized, from that person. You are deeply connected to anyone you have loved and lost. What has become of you because you have given and received love will last forever; the changes that are taking place in you are embedded in the very essence of your being.

You have loved from the outside in, and now you must learn to mourn from the inside out.

I thank you for taking the time to read and reflect on the words that make up this book. My hope is that this resource helps you continue to honor the reality that love doesn't stop when someone you are deeply connected to dies. May this book offer you something for your head, your heart, and your spirit.

If you find this book helpful, consider dropping me a note (drwolfelt@centerforloss.com) about how your love goes on and how you have been transformed by the loves and losses that have shaped your life.

Communion

"We are all mirrors unto one another. Look into me and you will find something of yourself, as I will of you."

—Walter Rinder

Love is a sacred partnership of communion with another human being. You take each other in, and even when you are apart, you are together. Wherever you go, you carry the person inside you.

Communion means the sharing or exchanging of intimate thoughts and feelings, especially on a spiritual level. When two people love one another, they are connected. They are entwined.

The word "communion" comes from the Old French *comuner*, which means "to hold in common." Note that this is different than "to *have* in common." You may have very little in common with another person yet love them wholeheartedly. Instead, you *hold* things in common—that is, you consciously choose to share one another's lives, hopes, and dreams. You hold her heart, and she holds yours.

This experience of taking another person inside your heart is beyond definition and defies analysis. It is part of the mystery of love. Love has its own way with us. It knocks on our hearts and invites itself in. It cannot be seen, but we realize it has happened. It cannot be touched, yet we feel it.

When someone we love dies, then, we feel a gaping hole inside us. I have companioned hundreds of mourners who have said to me, "When she died, I felt like part of me died, too." In what can feel like a very physical sense, something that was inside us now seems missing. We don't mourn those who die from the outside in; we mourn them from the inside out.

The absence of the person you love wounds your spirit, creates downward movement in your psyche, and transforms your heart. Yet, even though you may feel there is now a "hole inside you," you will also come to know (if you haven't already) that those you love live on in your heart. You remain in communion with those you love forever and are inextricably connected to them for eternity.

Yes, you will grieve the person's absence and need to express your feelings of grief. You must mourn. You must commune with your grief and take it into your heart, embracing your many thoughts and feelings. When you allow yourself to fully mourn, over time and with the support of others who care about you, you will come to find that the person you lost does indeed still live inside you.

Love abides in communion—during life and after death. And mourning is communion with your grief. With communion comes understanding, meaning, and a life of richness.

ASK YOURSELF:

• Did you feel in communion with the person who died when he or she was alive?

• Can you relate to what many mourners say: "When he (or she) died, I felt like part of me died too"? If so, why do you think that is?

• How are you mourning from the inside out?

• In what ways are you in communion with your grief?

• Do you still feel in communion with the person who died?

"Duration alone does not bring this miracle, but unremitting devotion does."

—Hugh and Gayle Prather

"If you place two living heart cells from different people in a Petri dish, they will in time find and maintain a third and common beat."

— Molly Vass

"Love is of all passions the strongest, for it attacks simultaneously the head, the heart, and the senses."

—Lao Tzu

"In the sweetness of friendship let there be laughter and sharing of pleasures. For in the dew of little things, the heart finds its morning and is refreshed."

—Khalil Gibran

"The best and most beautiful things in the world cannot be seen or even touched— they must be felt with the heart."

—Helen Keller

"When you fish for love, bait with your heart, not your brain."

—Mark Twain

Greater

than the

SUM OF ITS PARTS

*"The most
important
business of
life is love,
or maybe it's
the only one."*

—Stendhal

When you love another person, it can feel like one plus one equals three.

I'm sure you've heard the saying, "The whole is greater than the sum of its parts." Love is like that. Two people can come together and form a partnership that enables each person to be "more" in so many ways.

Here's another way to think about this idea: Love is like an orchestra. You may be a clarinet—a strong, fine wind instrument all by yourself. But when you surround yourself with other instruments, each of whom do the work of carrying their own parts and practicing their own music, together, as a group, you can blow the doors off the place.

I much prefer this expansive concept of love over the long-held reductionist belief that "two become one." If two become one, both participants in the relationship are diminished. Conversely, what truly feeds the soul of a loving relationship is expansion, mutual-nurturance, and growth.

Without doubt, being part of a synergistic, two-makes-three relationship, requires a conscious commitment. Did your relationship with the person who died feel enhancing or diminishing?

In synergistic relationships, there has to be space and encouragement to be real and authentic. Were you empowered to be your true self or disempowered to be something you were not? Did your two make three, or did your two make you less than one? If so, perhaps you are now faced with mourning what you never had but wished you did. How human is that?

If, on the other hand, your relationship with the person who died made you greater than the some of your parts, what happens now that one of you is gone? You may feel diminished. You may feel empty. You may feel "less than." Your self-identity may even seem to shrink as you struggle with your changing roles. If you are no longer a wife or a husband (or a mother or a father, or a sister or a brother, or a daughter or a son), what are you?

Also, the experience of mourning can feel piecemeal—a cry here, a burst of anger there; a deep sadness today, a crush of guilt tomorrow. You might feel a sense of disorientation from the scattered and ever-changing nature of your grief.

But when you trust in the process of grief and you surrender to the mystery, you will find that mourning, like love, is also greater than the sum of its parts. Leaning into your grief and always erring on the side of expressing rather than inhibiting or ignoring your thoughts and feelings—no matter how random and disjointed they might seem some days—will bring you to a place of transformation. You will not just be different from the person you were before the death. You will be greater. Your experience of love and grief will create a changed you, a you who has not only survived but who has learned to thrive again in a new form and in a new way.

> *"Never is true love blind, but rather brings an added light."*
>
> —Phoebe Cary

And just as love connects you to others, so should grief. You need the listening ears and open hearts of others as you express your thoughts and feelings about the death. You need the support of others as you mourn.

Yes, love and grief are both greater than the sum of their parts. The lesson I take from this is that whenever you engage fully and openly in life, experiencing both the joys and the sorrows head-on, you are living the life you were meant to live.

ASK YOURSELF:

- *In your relationship with the person who died, how were you together greater than the sum of your parts? (And if you weren't, why?)*

- *How is your self-identity changing as a result of this death?*

- *Does your mourning feel random or piecemeal? How so?*

- *In what ways can you feel your grief symptoms and experiences adding up to a greater whole?*

- *Are you trusting and opening yourself to the journey that is grief? How?*

"No one can whistle a symphony. It takes an orchestra to play it."

—H.E. Luccock

"Synergy is the highest activity of life; it creates new untapped alternatives; it values and exploits the mental, emotional, and psychological differences between people."

—Stephen Covey

"Alone we can do so little; together we can do so much."

—Helen Keller

"My humanity is bound up in yours, for we can only be human together."

—Desmond Tutu

"Accept the things to which fate binds you, and love the people with whom fate brings you together, but do so with all your heart."

—Marcus Aurelius

Uniqueness

"Telling a story, especially about ourselves, can be one of the most personal and intimate things we can do."

—Richard Stone

How amazing is it that there will be no love exactly like the one you shared? No one will say your name just as this person did. No one will touch you in precisely the same way this person did. No one will smile at you in exactly the same way this person did. Your unique love was and is truly divine.

You rejoiced together in the unique pleasures of your relationship. What about this person and your relationship brightened your day? What made your heart glad to be with him? What did she bring to the dance of your life together?

Love unites us through shared experiences and open communication. How did you share experiences like birthdays, holidays, and anniversaries with your loved person? How did you celebrate the cycles of your love? How did you survive the crises and difficult times you lived through together? What were the uniquely good times and the uniquely bad times?

Authentic love invites each of us to embrace our own uniqueness, the uniqueness of the person who died, and the uniqueness of the relationship we shared. This recognition of the uniqueness is what made your relationship have energy and connection. This allowed you to share your love in an instinctual way that expressed a depth of feelings beyond words.

Of course, all of the unique qualities that defined your relationship in life will now also define your grief journey. So many factors go into determining the shape and depth of your loss: the circumstances of the death; your personality; the personality of the person who died; the measure of attachment between you; your past experiences with loss; your cultural and religious background; your gender; and many others. Just as your love was unique, so will be your grief.

Love is never the same twice and neither is grief. Each is a one-of-a-kind story, a snowflake in the history of humanity. Part of your work now is to embrace your story, even as it continues to unfold and evolve into something ever-new.

In fact, after someone you love dies, the creation of renewed meaning and purpose in your life requires that you "re-story" your life. As you know, your grief experience is unique and personal. Although even the most compassionate person cannot completely comprehend what this is like for you, you will find comfort and support when you

"The wounds of the past must be tended by more than the frantic activity of getting on with it."

— Oriah Mountain Dreamer

surround yourself with people who will honor your story of love and loss.

The thoughts and feelings that bubble up when someone loved dies often feel heavy and overpowering. Expressing what this experience is like for you—telling the story of your love and your grief—is one way to release the pain that has pierced your heart. Expressing yourself can bring some light into the midst of the dark because it will allow you to feel heard, understood, and loved.

Find people who make you feel safe and will truly listen—who will let you share without trying to fix, take way, or distract you from what you are feeling. If telling your story is difficult for you, take time to write it out and then share it with someone. Consider drawing or making something that represents what your grief journey feels like. Perhaps you can communicate your story through art instead of words with someone who is able to simply take in what you are communicating. Share your story in whatever way feels natural to you.

"You have a unique message to deliver, a unique song to sing, a unique act of love to bestow."

—John Powell

Because stories of love and loss take time, patience, and unconditional love, they serve as powerful antidotes to a modern society that is all too often preoccupied with getting you to "let go," "move on," and "find closure." Whether you share your story with a friend, a family member, a coworker, or a fellow traveler in grief whom you've met through a support group, having others bear witness to the telling of your unique story is one way to go backward on the pathway to eventually going forward.

Honoring your one-of-a-kind story invites you to slow down, turn inward and create the sacred space to do so. Having a place to have your love story honored allows you to embrace what needs to embraced and come to understand that you can and will come out of the dark and into the light. You heal yourself as you tell the tale. This is the awesome power of the love story.

"This moment, this day, this relationship, this life are all exquisite, unique, and unrepeatable."

—Daphne Rose Kingma

ASK YOURSELF:

• *In what ways was your relationship unique or special? Make a list. Be specific.*

• *Have you found some people who are willing and able to help you "re-story" your life? If so, who are they and why do you feel safe with them?*

• *As you go backward and honor your love story, what is that experience like for you?*

• *Have you found yourself connecting with other people who also need to tell their love stories? If so, what is that like for you?*

"Relationships are about trying.
And learning.
And working.
And playing.
And trying.
And doing.
And being.
And loving."

—Gregory J.P. Godek

"Never forget that you are one of a kind. Never forget that if there weren't any need for you in all your uniqueness to be on this earth, you wouldn't be here in the first place. And never forget, no matter how overwhelming life's challenges and problems seem to be, that one person can make a difference in the world. In fact, it is always because of one person that all the changes in the world come about. So be that person."

—Buckminster Fuller

BEING IN

Orbit

"Love consists in this... that two solitudes protect and touch and greet each other."

—Rainer Maria Rilke

I once heard someone say, "You don't *fall* in love, you *orbit* in love." Consider yourselves two separate planets, he said, each with your own gravity and path, sharing a part of the universe in which you orbit around each other, independent but with intertwining orbits.

I find much wisdom in his words because in space, the gravity of attraction and the impetus of separate momentum *together* are what create an orbit.

Are you familiar with the yin-yang symbol? It represents the synergetic combination of opposites. In it, light and darkness fit together in graceful curves—each containing a circle of the other within itself. Intertwined, they form a perfect circle, which itself is a universal symbol of infinity and wholeness.

Yes, loving relationships are a mysterious force between two universes. Just as planets are connected in the cosmic forces of synchronistic orbiting, the lives of two who love each other are interconnected. Each individual in the relationship has his own interests, experiences, friendships, and philosophies, yet the two share other important things, such as common values, senses of humor, and even genetics in cases of family members.

But what happens to the synchronistic orbit of love when one of the orbiting bodies is physically gone from sight? What do you do with the love that remains?

Society often tells us that we should not continue to stay connected to someone who is no longer alive. We are often told to "put the past in the past" and "move on," as if we can and should stop loving the person who died.

Yet, it is in coming to understand the reality that love *doesn't* die that we create meaning to live into the future. I believe that continuing to love and mourning the death are not mutually exclusive. Actually, integrating loss into our lives means having the courage to continue to love, even in the face of loss.

Yes, we may feel like we have this love but no place to put it. In part, grief becomes our experience of not having our love received. And yet, we continue to love because anyone we have ever

"There is no me without a you, no father and husband and lover without the counterpart of child, of wife, and beloved."

—I. Edward Kiev

"Real love stories don't have endings."

—Gregory J.P. Godek

internalized, or taken in, is never truly lost. Even in acknowledging the loss, something soulful remains. The person has become a part of the fabric of our being.

As long as we are alive, we have both the instinct and the capacity to continue to love, even when someone is no longer a part of our daily reality. We can authentically mourn this profound loss even as we consciously value what we have taken in from this person we continue to love. To do this demands that we challenge many of the notions that our society projects about grief and loss: That we must "let go" and "resolve" our grief. That what we can no longer see is gone. That what we can no longer touch doesn't live on. That people who love each other are irrevocably parted by death.

In truth, we could not stop loving even if we wanted to. Love never dies. And so we must give new form to the orbit of love. Our grief and mourning become the container for what we have lost only in the physical sense. Our orbit wobbles and drifts for a while as we do the hard work of mourning, yet eventually we find a new groove, a new path in which to orbit. We transform that love into loving memory and carry it with us for the rest of our lives—and beyond.

Such conversion is not denial but transformation. The challenge is

"Speak to me of the stars and the heavens, and all of creation, and I will speak to you of love."

—Anonymous

to bring those who have died into our future orbit in a way that honors them. This, and only this, is the suitable incorporation of loss into the celebration of life. If there is no experience of loss, there was nothing of significance. If there was something of significance, it remains with us. Now, the quest becomes to travel through life still and always intertwined with the person who died yet open to new paths, relationships, and orbits that will bring continued meaning to each of our days until we, too, vanish into the heavens.

"Life is eternal and love is immortal. And death is only a horizon, and a horizon is nothing save the limit of our sight."

—Rossiter W. Raymond

ASK YOURSELF:

• *Were you in orbit in your relationship?*

• *How do we best honor those who go before us by making their contribution to our lives conscious, live with that value in an "on- purpose" way, and go on living until we die?*

• *Have you been told you need to "put the past in the past?" If so, what does that feel like for you?*

• *What do you think of the idea that someone precious we have loved is never lost?*

"You and I will meet again. When we're least expecting it, one day in some far off place, I will recognize your face. I won't say goodbye my friend, for you and I will meet again."

—Tom Petty

Death is nothing at all.
I have only slipped away to the next room.
I am I and you are you.
Whatever we were to each other,
That, we still are.

Life means all that it ever meant.
It is the same that it ever was.
There is absolute unbroken continuity.
Why should I be out of mind
because I am out of sight?

I am but waiting for you.
For an interval.
Somewhere. Very near.
Just around the corner.

All is well.

— Henry Scott Holland

Presence

*"Life is now.
There was
never a time
when your life
was not now,
nor will there
ever be."*

—Eckhart Tolle

When we first begin to love someone, in those heady early days of love, we delight in simply spending time with the person. We "live in the now" with her, focusing on her face and her voice. We notice her hands and the way she moves. Our senses are heightened and we tend to be generally more aware of textures and tastes, sights and sounds and smells.

Love is a state of being that can give us the gift of presence. Temporarily.

As love matures, we almost always slip back into our habit of living in the past or the future. We go through the motions of our daily routines, yet our minds are on what happened last week or last year or on what we expect (or worry) might happen tomorrow.

Many people believe that the key to inner bliss is learning to always remain in the present. Spiritual practices such as meditation and focused breathing are intended to teach us to focus on the now and quiet our monkey minds, which chatter at us about the past and future and constantly swing from subject to subject.

Early grief, like early love, has a habit of refocusing us on the pain of now. When someone we love dies, it can feel as if the world stops. We feel as if we are standing still or moving in slow motion. There may be times we don't even feel like getting our feet out of bed because the weight of our grief feels too heavy or cumbersome. The weight of grief is a reminder to us that what our bodies and souls need most right now is to slow down, stop, rest, and just be.

"Things come suitable to their time."

—Enid Bagnold

During this naturally difficult time, tell yourself that it is okay to slow down, to not do so much, and to allow yourself to rest and go into retreat for at least a little while. Listen to your body, your mind and your spirit begging you to lighten your load. It can be so difficult to slow down in a culture that wants you to "move forward."

Your grief is also telling you that it needs your attention, that it needs you to live in the present with it and acknowledge it for what it is. Being aware of your thoughts and feelings and embracing them as they surface will allow them, over time and with the support of others, to pass through you. Denying or distracting yourself from your grief, on the other hand, will only delay and complicate your healing.

Even as you are learning to live in the present with your grief, you can, at the same time, learn to live in the present with all that is good in your life. Take a walk and feel the sun on your face and the breeze in your hair. Feel your muscles as they move you through time and space. Hug someone you love and pay close attention to the sensations in your arms and chest. Play your favorite music, close your eyes, and listen, really listen, to the instrumentation. Have a conversation with someone you care about and hold her in your gaze, aware of her body language and tone of voice as well as her words.

As you move through grief, you just might learn that faster is often not better. In fact, the slowness of living in the present second to second, minute to minute, may be just the right speed for your life for now—and maybe even for the rest of your days.

"Nothing is worth more than this day".

—Johann Wolfgang von Goethe

In part, others encourage you to speed through your grief out of their own sense of helplessness and discomfort with witnessing someone else in pain. They desperately want to reduce the hurt you feel, which is impossible, so instead they encourage you to act as if it's not there. This only creates the illusion that you are free of it, because grief remains despite any attempts to suppress or ignore it. In fact, in some ways, it gives grief permission to stick around and fester, because you are not giving it the attention it needs to soften.

Even the most compassionate other may not understand the role of the pain and grief and the importance of allowing you to sit in the wound of your grief as you move toward hope and healing. The more others push you to quickly move forward and you listen, the more you will have a tendency to feel you are doing something wrong in your grief journey. Yet, the faster you try to "get through" your grief, the longer it will actually take. Fast, rushed, hurried movements do not allow your thoughts and emotions to fully express themselves across time in "doses" as you do the work of mourning.

> *"The most precious gift we can offer others is our presence. When mindfulness embraces those we love, they will bloom like flowers."*
>
> —Thich Nhat Hanh

Remind yourself that this journey is not about "getting over" your grief. Rather, it is a journey that helps you to reconcile and integrate all that has changed in you and in your world. Walking—deliberately, consciously, intentionally, and *presently*—through grief helps you give this loss a little space in your heart to reside so that it does not consume every moment of every day.

Eventually, if you mourn authentically and have the support of others who care about you, you may find that the art of presence in grief has re-taught you much about the art of presence in life and love. In this way, your grief journey may well bring you back around to love again.

ASK YOURSELF:

- What do you remember about the sensation of being in the moment with the person who died in the early days of your relationship?

- How did your ability to live in the now with this person change as your love matured?

- What does your grief feel like today?

- What are your body, your mind, and your spirit telling you about the need to go slow right now?

- Which physical symptoms are you experiencing that might be serving as invitations to go slow in your grief journey?

- Are some people giving you messages to speed up your grief? If so, why do you think this is?

- What happens when you sit still for two minutes and use your senses to be aware of all the sights, sounds, smells, tastes, and textures around you? Try it now.

"Love...Force it and it disappears. You cannot will love, nor even control it. You can only guide its expression. It comes or it goes according to those qualities in life that invite it or deny its presence."

—David Seabury

*"You must live
in the present,
launch yourself
on every wave,
find your eternity
in each moment.
Fools stand on
their island
opportunities
and look toward
another land.
There is no other
land, there is
no other life but
this."*

—Henry David
Thoreau

Trust

"*We need to acknowledge that this experience of grief and mourning is part of the soul's life.*"

—Thomas Moore

Loving relationships are built or destroyed on trust. Trust is anchored in congruity, commitment, and the alignment of your actions with your words. For love to flourish, we must be able to consistently count on the person we love to mean what they say and do what they promise.

Trusting someone you love invites you to openly be yourself. If there is a lack of trust, you naturally feel the need to retract, to defend, or even to obscure your authentic self. The true you goes into hiding when trust is absent. By contrast, trust allows you to be free and genuinely express who you are.

Deep trust and faith in each other often develop over time. Each time an agreement is honored, each time someone comes home when he says he will, each time she supports you through challenging times, trust strengthens and grows. On the other hand, if you encounter a lack of trustworthiness in someone you love, you can be shaken to the very core.

Of course, trust and vulnerability go hand in hand. When you trust someone, you open yourself to the fullness of life and love. Yet at the same time, opening yourself makes you vulnerable. And now you are experiencing the painful repercussions of vulnerability. You are, as they say, paying the piper. You took the risk of opening your heart and soul to another, you loved fully and deeply...and then the unthinkable happened. The person died.

But the keys to love also unlock healing in grief: trust and openness. Just as you opened your heart to love, you must open your heart to mourn. Yes, our hearts serve as our "well of reception" for both feelings of love and feelings of grief.

> *"We are healed of a suffering only by experiencing it to the full."*
>
> —Marcel Proust

It may be difficult to open your heart right now. Your heart may be so filled with pain that opening it feels impossible. But the inability to open your heart is what blocks authentic mourning, and blocked mourning keeps you in darkness.

When someone you love dies, your heart and mind are flooded with emotion. You cannot believe that the person you love will no longer physically be part of your days. At times the hurt runs so deep that you may want to put up walls and protect your vulnerable heart from any more pain. You may fear losing love again.

Protecting your heart literally by taking care of yourself is one of the best things you can do when you are mourning the death of someone loved. Eat well. Exercise. Get enough rest. But protecting your heart metaphorically by retreating from the love of others is not something that will help you heal. Holding love at arm's length means you may be missing out on the opportunity to have loving support, genuine caring, and authentic warmth at a time when you need them most.

This loss is a reminder that love is precious. It is something you want to experience as much and as often as possible. Don't turn away from the support or love that others have to offer, even in the face of fear of more loss. Keep your heart open to love, and hope and light will find their way in, no matter how overwhelmed by grief you may feel.

Another way to think about opening your heart to grief and trusting in the process of mourning is the idea of surrender. The alternative to carrying your grief around inside you forever is allowing yourself to surrender to the pain, which, in effect, honors the love.

Surrender teaches us that when we stop resisting and surrender to a situation exactly as it is, things begin to change. Surrender is, in part, about accepting the reality that we are unable to stop or control unwelcome change in our lives.

"Grief symptoms are expressions of a desire to integrate loss into our lives. Instead of denying or trying to change them, we are better served to surrender to the 'special needs' they represent."

—Alan. D. Wolfelt

Resistance or protest is an instinctive defense mechanism we use to push away or deny our pain, to naturally protect ourselves from feelings of loss and grief.

When we surrender, we release attachment to how we feel our lives should be and instead allow ourselves to be present to our lives exactly as they are. When we surrender, we stop trying to control what we cannot control. By allowing ourselves to surrender to the energies of grief, we create conditions for something new to arise from within—out of the dark and into the light!

> *"You are love itself—when you are not afraid."*
>
> —Sri Nisargadatta Maharaj

The word "feeling" originates from the Indo-European root that means "touch." To feel is to activate our capacity to be touched and changed by experiences we encounter along life's path—in this instance, the death of someone in our lives.

Our feelings reflect the way we perceive ourselves and the world around us. If we shut them down—if we deny, repress, or inhibit them—we risk being among the "living dead." If we lose touch with our feelings, we have no true awareness of life.

The purpose of mourning is to allow feelings to move through us in ways that integrate them into our lives. To integrate grief into our lives requires that we allow ourselves to be "touched" by what we experience. When we cannot feel our feelings, we become closed in our ability to use them or be changed by them, and instead of experiencing movement, we become "stuck." If we become stuck, not only do we struggle to identify what we are feeling, we often have difficulty expressing feelings to people around us.

Our hearts are moved entirely by what they have perceived. In allowing ourselves to befriend our feelings, we discover the natural, organic place of grief in our lives. I truly believe that place is in our hearts, right beside our capacity to love and be loved.

The word "emotion" literally means "energy in motion." To be authentic with our emotions is to have them work for us instead of against us. To do that requires that we put our emotions into motion through befriending them. Open and honest mourning anchored in feeling our feelings is an opportunity to embrace our open hearts in ways that invite us to reignite our capacity to laugh again, to live again, and yes, to love again!

ASK YOURSELF:

- *Have you been allowing yourself to feel your feelings of loss and grief? If so, how? If not, why not?*

- *Do you ever find yourself trying to "think" through your grief rationally? If so, why do you think that is, and is it helpful?*

- *Which feelings have you had most recently in your grief journey? Describe them.*

"To love at all is to be vulnerable. Love anything, and your heart will certainly be wrung and possibly broken. If you want to make sure of keeping it intact, you must give your heart to no one, not even to an animal. Wrap it carefully round with hobbies and little luxuries; avoid all entanglements; lock it up safe in the casket or coffin of your selfishness. But in that casket—safe, dark, motionless, airless—it will change. It will not be broken; it will become unbreakable, impenetrable, irredeemable."

— C.S. Lewis

Intention

AND ACTION

"*Love is not a feeling. Love is an action, an activity. Genuine love implies commitment and the exercise of wisdom. True love is an act of will that often transcends ephemeral feelings of love. It is correct to say, 'Love is as love does.'*"

—M. Scott Peck

Love is a verb. So is mourning.

Of course, love is a feeling (or even a state of being), but it is a feeling made possible by action. To truly love someone means to act on her behalf in compassionate, selfless, and kind ways. In a romantic relationship, feelings of love and desire may spring up seemingly out of nowhere, but they falter and fade without the sustaining power of action. A backrub, a home-cooked meal, a surprise get-away, a daily "I love you." These are the kinds of gestures that not only demonstrate love but, over time, actually create it anew, over and over again.

Love is intention *plus* action.

Yes, relationships take work. Love is not passive but active. And now, your grief will also take work. It takes a true commitment to heal your grief. To heal in grief is to become whole again, to integrate your grief into your self and to learn to continue your changed life with fullness and meaning. Healing doesn't *happen* to you. You create it, slowly and over time, with the support of others.

First you must set your intention to heal. Intention is defined as being conscious of what you want to experience. A close cousin of "affirmation," it is using the power of positive thought to produce a desired result. With commitment and intention you can and will become whole again.

When you set your intention to heal, you make a true commitment to positively influence the course of your journey. You choose between being what I call a "passive witness" or an "active participant" in your grief. I'm sure you have heard the cliché "Time heals all wounds." Yet time alone has nothing to do with healing. Grief waits on welcome, not on time. To heal, you must be willing to learn about the mystery of the grief journey. It cannot be fixed or "resolved," it can only be "reconciled" through actively experiencing the multitude of thoughts and feelings.

This concept of intention-setting presupposes that your outer reality is a direct reflection of your inner thoughts and feelings. If you can mold some of your beliefs, you can influence your reality. Your beliefs have the power to help you heal. If you routinely remind yourself that you *will* survive this loss, you will set a course of divine momentum toward your healing.

"Love is a verb. Love—the feeling—is the fruit of love the verb or our loving actions. So love her. Sacrifice. Listen to her. Empathize. Appreciate. Affirm her."

—Stephen Covey

Action, then, picks up where intention-setting leaves off. Mourning is grief in action. Just as you took the love you felt inside and you expressed it through action in your relationship with the person who died, you must now take the grief you feel inside and express it through mourning.

How you choose to mourn is up to you. Talking to good listeners is one way. Writing in a journal is another. Attending a support group is a third. Other mourning activities include crying, creating art, getting physical (such as through dance or sports), engaging in spiritual practices (such as prayer or meditation), and actively remembering (such as creating a memory book or photo collage).

Set your intention to heal then, slowly and in doses, take actions that help you mourn the death. Set your intention to love, then take actions to nurture the meaningful relationships that still exist in your life. Set your intention to be present, then take actions to spend more and more time each day in the now. You get the idea. Intention plus action equals a life lived deeply and on-purpose.

"Believe that life is worth living, and your belief will help you create the fact."

—William James

"Follow your instinct. That's where true wisdom manifests itself."

—Oprah Winfrey

ASK YOURSELF:

- *Do you agree that love is a verb? Why or why not?*

- *How did your love relationship demonstrate the power of intention plus action?*

- *In grief, how you have set your intention to heal?*

- *What are some ways in which you are actively expressing—mourning—your loss?*

- *Have you experienced any examples in your own life of the power of intention plus action?*

"Live with intention. Walk to the edge. Listen hard. Practice wellness. Play with abandon. Laugh. Choose with no regret. Appreciate your friends. Continue to learn. Do what you love. Live as if this is all there is."

—Mary Anne Radmacher

Joy

"Think of all the beauty that's still left in and around you and be happy."

—Anne Frank

Oh what joy there can be in love. Have you ever felt greater joy than when you first held your beloved's hand or gazed into your newborn's eyes? The joy of living in orbit with someone you love is unmatched by any other experience in life.

So after the person you love dies, it is natural to question if you will ever be joyful again. Grief results in a natural muting of your divine spark—that which gives your life meaning and purpose.

When someone you love dies, it can feel as if the loss drains every ounce of happiness right out of you. Loss leaves you feeling empty, weary, and depleted. Yet, even when it feels as if happiness is gone, you can be assured it is still there, waiting to be rediscovered.

But where is it and how do you find it again? First, understand that happiness is not something you can search for and find in the external world. It doesn't exist in any possession you own. It doesn't live in any particular achievement you have reached. It isn't related to your socioeconomic status. It cannot be handed to you by any person in your life. Rather, happiness is something that exists *within* you. Only *you* have the capacity to find it, feel it, and nurture it toward its full potential. Only *you* can cultivate from within yourself the intense happiness we call joy.

Happiness is a friend of hope, and often the two are inseparable. Hope is an expectation of a good that is yet to be. Rediscovering happiness and hope in big and small ways will uplift and energize you. It will allow you to live with expression and animation as you walk through the world.

> *"Stretch out your hand and take the world's wide gift of joy and beauty."*
>
> —Corinne Roosevelt Robinson

When you carry happiness, it shows! It draws others in. On the contrary, when you feel sadness and gloom, it holds people at arm's length. And although no one can make you happy, when you bump into someone who radiates happiness, it can help you reconnect with the happiness that is hidden by the clouds of your grief. The next time you see someone laughing or being playful, stop and notice that you are bumping into happiness. Reflect on and remember some of the things that once brought laughter and play into your life.

If you have to, force yourself to play now and then. When you play, you rekindle the child in you. You free yourself from your responsibilities and burdens and may even remember how to embrace joy and have fun. Remember how I said love is a verb? So is play. Play is a choice you make to spend time participating in activities just because they're fun or entertaining. And often, it is when we play that we express our most authentic selves. As you play, you just might find your way back to your divine spark.

When loss enters your life it is also natural to question if you will ever experience gratitude again. After all, gratitude is something you feel when things are going well, and your time of grief is not such a time. Gratitude is what is expressed when you appreciate what is happening in your life, and appreciation is not likely something you feel in the aftermath of this loss.

Though it may seem impossible to feel gratitude at the same time as grief, the potential for gratitude remains. You are surrounded by people and things that are special to you. Identifying and acknowledging what you appreciate right now is more important than ever.

"Remember that not to be happy is not to be grateful."

—Elizabeth Carter

Take a moment to look around and discover where you can practice gratitude. Look at your relationships. Which living person or people are you grateful for? Look around where you live. What brings you comfort in your home? Look at the actions of others. What has someone done to offer you support? Look at yourself. What qualities do you have that those around you admire?

If these reflections do not help you discover what you are grateful for despite your grief, simply try another approach. Gratitude can grow when you try calling it forth in situations you might not normally be grateful for. Practice expressing gratitude in your mind or out loud for things that are so ordinary that gratitude doesn't even cross your mind when you encounter them. Consider some of the following everyday (yet at the same time miraculous) things: nature, your body and mind, children, your favorite companion animal, the person who died, your courage and faith, God's love for you.

You can and will rediscover gratitude, happiness and yes, even joy. No matter the circumstances and events that may challenge you, life is replete with miracles and goodness.

"Each day comes bearing its own gifts. Untie the ribbons."

—Ruth Ann Schabacker

ASK YOURSELF:

• *What makes you happy, even as you experience the dark clouds of grief?*

• *What used to bring you joy? How can you set your intention and take action to rekindle that joy?*

• *Who are some of the people in your life that you have gratitude for and why?*

• *What are you actively doing to help yourself rediscover happiness and gratitude in your life?*

"Appreciation is the highest form of prayer, for it acknowledges the presence of good wherever you shine the light of your thankful thoughts."

— Alan Cohen

"Pleasure
is always
derived from
something
outside you,
whereas joy
arises from
within."

—Eckhart Tolle

"Weeping may
endure for a
night, but joy
cometh in the
morning."

—Psalm 30:5

"...keep
knocking,
and the joy
inside will
eventually
open a
window and
look out to see
who's there."

—Rumi

"Joy is our
goal, our
destiny. We
cannot know
who we are
except in joy.
Not knowing
joy, we do
not know
ourselves."

—Marianne
Williamson

Hope

"When the world says, 'Give up,' Hope whispers, 'Try it one more time.'"

—Anonymous

We have discussed the importance of striving to live mindfully in the present. The power of now is that as your life continues to unfold one second at a time, you embrace it *as it happens* and learn to live with appreciation and joy for the miracles inherent in every moment.

But what about hope? Hope is an expectation that something positive is coming, that the future holds goodness and happiness and love. When your present and past are made painful by grief, thank goodness for hope. "Hope is that feeling you have that the feeling you have isn't permanent," famously said playwright Jean Kerr.

In your loving relationship with the person who died, you enjoyed the present and you also looked forward to the months and years to come. You were present and you were also hopeful. Wasn't that a wonderful combination? You can and will regain this synergy of present and future if you commit yourself to fully and openly mourning the loss.

Mourning can, and often does, invite you to question the meaning and purpose of life before you can create new hope. You recognize that so many things in your daily life have changed—your plans, your dreams, your concerns, and your roles. You may discover yourself searching for a reason to go on living in the face of this loss. You are confronted with trying to find some sense of meaning when you may be feeling alone and discouraged.

"Hope is like the sun, which, as we journey toward it, casts the shadow of our burden behind us."

—Samuel Smiles

Many hundreds of people in grief have said to me variations on, "I feel so hopeless" or "I am not sure I can go on living." Like yours, the losses that have touched their lives have naturally muted, if not extinguished, their divine sparks—that internal energy that gives meaning and purpose to life.

Before loss entered your life, you may have taken your divine spark for granted. With loss and grief comes a sense of being out of harmony with the world around you. You begin to learn more about who you are under these conditions of suffering and pain. You begin to recognize how precious your divine spark is and the importance of caring for it. Lost love often results in awareness that your divine spark needs self-care and lots of nourishment.

Practicing good self-care doesn't mean you are feeling sorry for yourself, being selfish, or being self- indulgent; rather, it means you are creating conditions that allow you integrate the death into your heart and soul and rediscover hope for living. In nurturing yourself, in allowing yourself the time and loving attention you need to journey safely and deeply through grief, you will find meaning in your continued living.

As time distorts and the loss cuts you off from your "normal" way of being in the world, it is important to remember that above all, self-nurturance is about self-acceptance. When you recognize that self-care begins with you, you no longer think of those around you as being responsible for your well-being. At the same time, you come to appreciate the importance of being connected to others. When you allow yourself to accept outside support and compassion from family, friends, and even strangers, you feel more in harmony with the world around you. Your capacity to receive this loving support helps restore your sense of hope!

"I find hope in the darkest of days, and focus in the brightest. I do not judge the universe."

—Dalai Lama

One way to bring hope into your life right now is to gently remind yourself that you will survive. Somehow. Some way. You don't have to foresee exactly how or why or when, but know that you will make it through to the other side of this. Let yourself whisper these hope-filled words, "I will survive." Begin each new day reminding yourself that you will survive.

As you do this, your broken heart will begin to heal. Your healing heart will be able to feel love, joy, and happiness again. Just as a physical wound on your body heals when you give it proper care and attention, when you take time to care for and attend to the painful emotional and spiritual wounds that are present in your life, you will find hope and healing.

Let hope in somehow, somewhere...and believe that you will survive. As you allow hope in, your renewed energy will be a gentle reminder that your divine spark is preparing for reignition.

"Love recognizes no barriers. It jumps hurdles, leaps fences, penetrates walls to arrive at its destination full of hope."

—Maya Angelou

ASK YOURSELF:

- *As you have learned about the concept of "divine spark," how would you describe yours right now?*

- *How are you doing with your self-care at this time?*

- *Are you accepting the hope that people around you are trying to give you? If so, how? If not, why not?*

"He who has health, has hope; and he who has hope, has everything."

—Thomas Carlyle

"Hope begins in the dark, the stubborn hope that if you just show up and try to do the right thing, the dawn will come. You wait, and watch, and work; you don't give up."

—Anne Lamott

"Everything that is done in the world is done by hope."

—Martin Luther

"Where there is no vision, there is no hope."

—George Washington Carver

"A very small degree of hope is sufficient to cause the birth of love."

—Stendhal

"Hope is the pillar that holds up the world."

—Anonymous

Transformation

*"Love is not
a mystery
to be solved.
It is an
experience
to be
savored."*

—Gregory J.P.
Godek

Transformation literally means "an entire change in form." Yes, loving relationships result in each of us becoming more than we ever would have on our own. Love transforms us and creates a new view of the world around us. Everything changes when we discover love.

In fact, another spiritual entity evolves when we go from being an "I" to a "we." The "we" radiates an invisible energy all around us. It is the magic by which one plus one equals three and the whole is greater than the sum of its parts. This spiritual connection inspires a sense of greater focus, which allows life experiences to take on greater meaning and purpose.

Listen to the transformative experiences love brought into one person's life: "I didn't realize I could feel this way. Everything looks and feels different. I have a new bounce to my step, a new outlook on each day...I can't wait to start each day, to see his face, to hear his voice. I'm thinking so clearly and I feel surrounded by joy."

Yes, love transforms our souls and sets us off on an amazing journey. The world begins to feel more considerate, gracious, and kind. We feel safe, held up, and even when it's dark, we feel light shining through.

Of course, loss is also transformative. The journey through grief in the aftermath of the death of someone you love is life-changing. I'm certain you have discovered that you have been transformed by your journey into grief. Many mourners have said to me, "I have grown from this experience. I am a different person."

> *"We cannot remain who we used to be, once love has made it over our walls and begun to change our hearts."*
>
> —Marianne Williamson

Now, don't take me the wrong way. Believe me, I understand that the growth resulted from something you would have preferred to avoid. While I have come to believe that our greatest gifts often come from our wounds, these are not wounds we masochistically go looking for. When others offer untimely comments like, "You'll grow from this," your right to be hurt, angry, or deeply sad is taken away from you.

Yet you are changing and growing nevertheless as a result of this loss. We as human beings can't help but be forever changed by the love and the death of someone in our lives. You may discover that you have developed new attitudes. You may be more patient or more sensitive to the feelings and circumstances of others, especially those suffering from loss. You may have new insights that guide the way you live your new life. You may have developed new skills or ways of viewing humankind or the world around you.

Your transformation probably also involves exploring your assumptions about life. Death invites this type of exploration. Your loss experiences have a tendency to transform your values and priorities. Every loss in life calls out for a new search for meaning, including a natural struggle with spiritual concerns, often transforming your vision of your God and your faith life.

"Relationship is not a project, it is a grace."

—Thomas Moore

Finally, your transformation may well include a need to do and be all you can be. In some ways, death loss seems to free the potential within. Questions such as "Who am I? What am I meant to do with my life?" often naturally arise during grief. Answering them inspires a hunt. You may find yourself searching for your very soul.

Yes, sorrow is an inescapable dimension of our human experience. We love and so we grieve. We rejoice and then we suffer. And in our suffering, we are transformed. While it hurts to suffer lost love, the alternative is apathy, or the inability to suffer, and it results in a lifestyle that avoids human relationship to avoid suffering.

Perhaps you have noticed that some people die a long time before they stop breathing. They have no more promises to keep, no more people to love, no more places to go. It is as if the souls of these people have already died. Don't let this happen to you. You have to continue to live not only for yourself but for the precious person in your life who has died—to work on his or her unfinished work and to realize his or her unfinished dreams.

What if the person who died could return to see what you are doing with your life? No matter how deep your grief or how anguished your soul, bereavement does not free you from your responsibility to live until you die. The gift of life is so precious and fragile. Choose life!

> "The only way to make sense out of change is to plunge into it, move with it, and join the dance."
>
> —Alan Watts

Tomorrow is here. It is waiting for you. You have many choices in living the transformation that grief has brought to your life. You can choose to visualize your heart opening each and every day. When your heart is open, you are receptive to what life brings you, both happy and sad. By staying open and present, you create a gateway to your healing.

When this happens you will know that the long nights of suffering in the wilderness have given way to a journey towards the dawn. You will know that new life has come as you celebrate the first rays of a new light and new beginning.

ASK YOURSELF:

• *In what ways did love transform your life?*

• *How is grief transforming your life?*

• *Are your assumptions, values, and priorities changing since the death? How or how not?*

• *In what ways are you living for the person who died?*

• *Would you say you have grown or are growing as a result of your grief?*

• *How will you live your new life even as you honor your past life and love?*

"Your relationship is a precious jewel. Not everyone has been given such a gift. Treasure it, hold it in your hand and up to the light, and let its extraordinary beauty open your heart and transform your life."

—Daphne Rose Kingma

"As far as inner transformation is concerned, there is nothing you can do about it. You cannot transform yourself, and you certainly cannot transform your partner or anybody else. All you can do is create a space for transformation to happen, for grace and love to enter."

—Eckhart Tolle

"A vision is not just a picture of what could be; it is an appeal to our better selves, a call to become something more."

—Rosabeth Moss Kanter

"Growth itself contains the germ of happiness."

—Pearl S. Buck

"If you begin to understand what you are without trying to change it, then what you are undergoes a transformation."

—Jiddu Krishnamurti

"We learn and grow and are transformed not so much by what we do but by why and how we do it."

—Sharon Salzberg

A FINAL
Word

"There is no remedy for love but to love more."

—Henry David Thoreau

When Carl Jung's wife died, he fell into a dark depression. For many months, he was depressed and inconsolable. Then, he had a dream. He was sitting in a theater all alone. He found himself drawn down to the front row, where he watched and waited. An orchestra pit was before him, representing the deep abyss he felt he was in. And then the curtain opened and he saw his wife, Emma, standing before him in a white dress, smiling at him, and he had an awakening: They were together, whether together or apart. He had not lost her, for she was still with him.

Yes, mourning lost love is an invitation to a maturation of consciousness. This maturation does not happen simply in the course of time, because grief waits on welcome, not on time. Instead, it requires engagement. Love and mourning can be a path to self-realization because in the unfolding of our hearts, we choose to acknowledge the death yet hold onto the love that continues.

> *"It is better to have loved and lost than never to have loved at all."*
>
> —Alfred Lord Tennyson

As I will explain below, I invite you to remember the power of AND as you move through the coming weeks and months. It may help you choose to be present, to live with intention and action, to seek joy and transformation. Whenever you feel stuck, whisper to yourself:

I am sad AND I am present to all that is good in my life.

I feel lost AND I am finding my way.

I miss him AND I choose joy.

I am bereft AND I am actively loving others in my life.

I grieve AND I love.

I love AND I mourn.

I wish you courage for the road ahead. Courage comes from the old French word for heart (*coeur*). You have within you a bold heart. You have the courage to openly and honestly mourn and to live and love fully until you die.

Godspeed. I hope we meet one day.